I0698502

ARGENTO PUBLISHING

THE ELEMENTS OF PYTHON
Learn to code by doing

Argento Publishing

Index

Introduction

Welcome to the fascinating world of programming! If you're reading these lines, it means you have a goal in mind: to learn a powerful and versatile language that allows you to apply your ideas and solutions to real-world problems. You're already off to a good start because, if nothing else, you're in the right place: at the beginning of your journey to discover the fundamentals of programming and unleash your full potential.

Whether you're a beginner with no experience or an experienced developer looking to expand your knowledge, this book will help you acquire the essential knowledge in just a few days to write and create your programs.

Our journey will start from the foundations. We will see and, more importantly, understand all the tools at our disposal to develop our work, such as variables, conditional statements, loops, functions... all the way to object-oriented programming and libraries.

Whether you're interested in developing applications or web services, or you want to explore machine learning, this is the foundation you've been looking for – the manual that will save you a lot of time and money spent on lengthy and complicated courses.

The lines of text have intentionally been kept concise, just like taking notes during a lecture. The important thing is understanding and categorizing the concepts behind the words. The informal language will allow you to grasp the topics covered quickly, and the continuous examples will clarify them better than any amount of talking could.

The innovative approach of this book will allow you to immediately put into practice every notion you learn. The numerous bites of knowledge and curiosities scattered throughout its pages can easily be tried out in the field.

All you need to do is open your development environment and keep this book next to your PC. For every page you turn, you'll find simple examples that I recommend you replicate on your keyboard right away.

The best way to learn something is to do it, immediately. True to this principle, this volume will teach you how to program while you're programming. There won't be study phases or pages to memorize while waiting to apply the concepts we're interested in. Instead, you'll continuously challenge yourself by creating increasingly complex programs.

Finally, I'd like to relieve you from the anxiety of memorizing all the keywords and parameters. It's not necessary. Or, rather, it will happen naturally. Don't worry if you have to program while flipping through the pages of the book at the beginning. Within a couple of weeks, with consistent practice, every construct, function, and syntax will naturally stick in your mind.

WHY CHOOSE PYTHON

There are many reasons why choosing Python is advantageous, both as a first language to learn and as a viable option for developing a program. The simplest reason is that **Python wins...** it wins when compared to other languages, and it wins when we think about what it can do well and in which areas it can be employed. Of course, depending on specific domains, there are more specialized languages that fit better for particular uses, but Python is capable of covering a wide range of situations and excelling in a variety of tasks.

It's versatile,

Python is a highly versatile programming language designed to solve a wide range of problems. It's used in many different applications, including data processing, web application development, scripting, scientific programming, machine learning, and much more. Furthermore, it's a dynamic language that allows for rapid and flexible development, making it ideal for startups and companies aiming to bring products to market quickly. Whatever the intended use, Python proves to be a solid choice.

Easy to approach,

Its simple and intuitive syntax makes Python a language that's easy to learn and use for programmers of all experience levels, with a gentle learning curve. Those who are familiar with conventional languages will feel comfortable, since they have access to all the structures they know, such as loops, conditional statements, arrays, etc., which are often easier to structure. Those approaching a programming language for the first time will find a solid starting point to explore the fundamental concepts of the development world.

powerful and expressive,

To put it simply, with a single line of Python code, you can achieve more compared to many other languages. This simple characteristic gives you numerous opportunities to develop advanced solutions and large-scale projects and also enabling developers to freely express themselves without being limited by intricate programming concepts.. Python is a sleek and elegant language, characterized by a simple, well-organized syntax optimized for readability and efficiency. It's designed to be easily modifiable and maintainable.

comprehensive,

Another Python's strong side is its extensive library ecosystem, providing all the tools needed to work with emails, web pages, databases, system calls, graphical interfaces, and much more. It can offer a great sense of security, especially at the beginning, not to get lost in installing packages and extensions and already having everything readily available.

and in great demand.

Finally, Python is one of the most popular and sought-after programming languages in the job market. Companies, big and small, are investing in Python-based solutions, offering a broad range of opportunities to develop skills and a career. As we've already said: **Python wins!**

LET'S GET STARTED!

In order to engage the content provided in this manual, just **install Python** and - optional but practically essential - **install an Integrated Development Environment** (IDE).

It doesn't matter which operating system you're using; both of the recommended tools have dedicated versions. It's possible that a certain resource is already pre-installed on some systems.

HOW TO INSTALL PYTHON

Andiamo sul sito https://www.python.org/downloads/ e selezioniamo il nostro sistema operativo: l' ultima versione di Python verrà installata. Se non si hanno particolari esigenze è sufficiente seguire l' installazione rapida.

La cosa <u>fondamentale</u> è **spuntare l' aggiunta di Python alla variabile d' ambiente PATH** (Add Python 3.11 to PATH).

Verificate la corretta installazione di Python sul vostro sistema aprendo il *prompt dei comandi* e digitando Python, si aprirà una *shell* interattiva (che non ci interessa, comunque).

Su Linux e Mac OS potreste dover usare il comando Python3.

Go to the website https://www.python.org/downloads/ and select your operating system: the latest version of Python will be installed. If you don't have specific requirements, simply follow the quick installation.

Be sure to check the option to **add Python to the PATH environment variable** (Add Python 3.11 to PATH).

Verify the correct installation of Python on your system by opening the *command prompt* and typing Python; an interactive *shell* will open (which we're not concerned with, however).

On Linux and Mac OS, you might need to use the command Python3.

HOW TO INSTALL IDE

An IDE is essentially a development environment that includes an editor and various tools for code analysis, testing, and debugging. There are various IDEs available online, each with its own strengths and weaknesses, both free and paid.

Per semplicità, sia di installazione che di utilizzo, scegliamo qui di installare **Pycharm di Jetbrains**, nella versione *Community Edition*, gratuita, che comunque si colloca a buon diritto nella top 5 degli IDE a livello mondiale.

For its simplicity in both installation and usage, let's choose to install **PyCharm by JetBrains**, *Community Edition*, which is free and rightfully ranks among the top 5 IDEs worldwide.

PyCharm is a very powerful tool for Python development. Here are some of its strong points that make it the best choice, at least in this phase:

1. PyCharm provides a powerful code auto-completion feature, also known as IntelliSense.

2. Offers robust integration with Python debuggers.

3. Includes many code analysis features, such as syntax checking and error detection.

4. Incorporates a wide range of integrated Python libraries.

5. Offers many customization options, such as theme selection and keyboard shortcut modification.

Go to the website https://www.jetbrains.com/pycharm/download/ and, if not automatically detected, select your operating system: the latest version of PyCharm will be installed. Simply follow the default installation, making sure to check the association with files having the *.py* extension.

Once PyCharm is launched, you can create a new project in a very intuitive way.

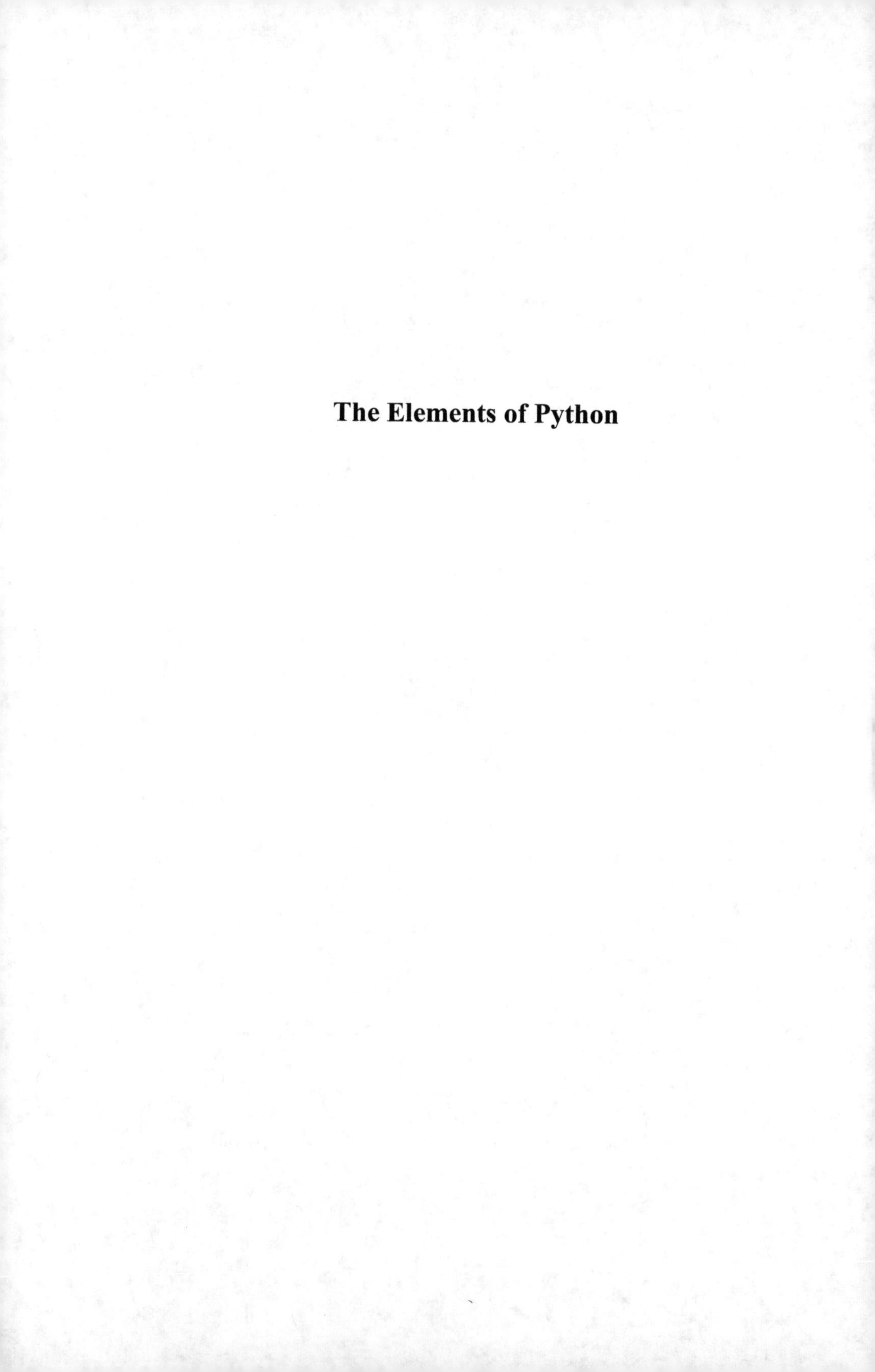

The Elements of Python

VARIABLES

Variables are data containers, like boxes, of different types, in which you can place various things of different types.

Assigning a value to a variable:

`x = 5` The variable **x** is filled with the numerical value **5**.

`x = "five"` The variable **x** is filled with the string **"five"**.

Assigning **multiple** values to **multiple** variables:

`x, y, z = 44, 20, 3` The variables **x**, **y**, and **z** are assigned the values **44**, **20**, and **3**.

`x = y = z = 32` **x** is equal to **y** which is equal to **z** which is equal to **32**.

`fruit = ["nuts", "pears", "apples"]` The variable (*list*) **fruit** is assigned the strings **"nuts"**, **"pears"** and **"apples"**.

The same 3 strings can be assigned to as many variables (*unpacking*):

`x, y, z = fruit` This will result in **x** = **"nuts"**, **y** = **"pears"** e **z** = **"apples"**.

DID YOU KNOW?

Variables can be written in many ways, using capital letters and underscores to provide them with a more straightforward readability:

`camelCase` *(starting with a lowercase letter and using uppercase letters to separate words),*
`PascalCase` *(All words, including the initial one, capitalized),*
`snake_case` *(the most handy: all in lowercase with words separated by hyphens." "_").*

DATA TYPES

There are various data types that we can use to fill a variable, each of them with different properties.

Let's consider a variable (**x**) that has been assigned any content.

type() function returns the data type.

`print(type(x))` To display one of the following strings:

CLASS	DATA TYPE
`str`	String – E.g: "apple".
`int`	Integer.
`float`	Floating-point number.
`bool`	Boolean (True or False)
`list`	List [ ] - E.g: ["hello", 13, False]
`tuple`	Tuple () - E.g: ("dog", "cat", "mouse")
`range`	Range - see below.
`dict`	Dictionary – see below.
`set`	Set {} - E.g: {"hello", 13, False}

E.g:

```
name = "Ivan"
year = 1981
print(type(name))
print(type(year))
```

Returns:

```
<class 'str'>
<class 'int'>
```

REMEMBER:
- *Boolean values are true and false. When using the Python language, it is mandatory to write them with uppercase initials: True and False.*
- *When writing numbers with decimals in variables, you must use a dot.*

CASTING

Converting the value of a variable into another data type.

For instance, attempting to add variables with different data types (typically, a number and a string) results in one of the following errors:

```
TypeError: unsupported operand type(s) for +: 'int' and 'str'
```

or

```
TypeError: can only concatenate str (not "int") to str
```

The following functions convert the data type:

str(5) ⇰ returns "5" (string)

int("5") ⇰ returns 5 (integer)

float("5") ⇰ returns 5.0 (floating-point number)

E.g:

```
x = 5
y = "5"
print(x + y)
```

Returns:

```
<unsupported operand type>
```

```
x = 5
y = "5"
print(x + int(y))
```

Returns:

```
10
```

DID YOU KNOW?

To define a string, you can use either single quotes (' ') or double quotes (" ").
Tripling the single quotes (''' ''') or double quotes (""" """) allows you to define multi-line strings.
E.g:

```
next event = "race"

next event = """ javelin
        throw """
```

STRINGS AS SEQUENCES OF CHARACTERS

A string can be thought of as the collection (or rather, the sequence) of the characters that compose it – including spaces, of course. An index identifies a specific element of this collection.

The syntax for accessing elements is `variable_name[index]`.

Example:

```
x = "choice"
print(x[2])
```
= o

It's worth to point out that the *index* starts from 0, not 1 as might be expected, following the pattern:

```
          c  h  o  i  c  e
index:    0  1  2  3  4  5
```

The function **len()** returns the number of elements (length) in an object.

```
x = "choice"
print(len(x))
```

Returns the length of **x**, which is 6.

I DO IT MYSELF:

```
For character in "computer"
        print(character)
```

*Let's write a simple **loop**, a repeating piece of code, which displays the letters of the word "computer".*
*We'll do it using a **for loop**, which we'll discuss later.*

➡ *__Len()__ is very interesting in combination with loops.*

➡ *A for loop is **an iterative control structure that repeats the execution of a portion of code.***

TAKING PART OF A STRING

We can extract portions of the content from a string using **indices** and **intervals**. In the syntax `variabile_name[index]`, we can use expressions instead of just a single *index*.

Let's go through some examples considering:

`x = "Hello my name is Miriam"`

With the syntax `x[0:3]` we will have: "`Hel`",

With the syntax `x[2:7]` we will have: "`llo m`",

With the syntax `x[3:23]` we will have: "`lo my name is Miriam`".

An interval (E.g. `0:3`) goes from the first number (0) up to, but excluding, the last, so: 0, 1, 2.

- If you omit the starting number, the interval will start from the beginning (0), so `x[0:3]` can be replaced with `x[:3]`.

- If you omit the ending number, the interval will go up to the end, so `x=[3:23]` can be replaced with `x[3:]`.

Negative indices

If an **index** has a negative value, counting starts from the end of the string, following this numbering: -1 (last letter), -2 (second-to-last letter), etc.

Let's take a few examples considering the same string:

`x = "Hello my name is Miriam"`

With the syntax `x[-4]` we will have: "`r`",

With the syntax `x[-4:]` we will have: "`riam`".

METHODS

With the syntax

```
string.method(optional_parameters)
```

we can perform numerous actions on strings, such as checks or modifications.

Let's go through some examples:

x.upper() = returns a string in uppercase: "*HELLO MY NAME IS MIRIAM*"
x.lower() = returns a string in lowercase : "*hello my name is miriam*"
x.swapcase() = swaps uppercase with lowercase : "*hELLO MY NAME IS mIRIAM*"
x.strip() = removes spaces from the beginning and end of the string.
x.replace("*letter1*", "*letter2*"**)** = replaces one letter with another.

The **format()** method can be used to combine strings and numbers, or strings and variables containing numerical values.

Example:

```
hello = "I am Lavinia and I am {}!"
print(hello.format(10))
```

Inserts **10** in place of the curly braces.

Returns:

```
I am Lavinia and I am 10!
```

Or:

```
x = 10
hello = "I am Lavinia and I am {}!"
print(hello.format(x))
```

Inserts **x** in place of the curly braces.

Returns:

```
I am Lavinia and I am 10!
```

It's possible to insert a series of values, just separate them with commas.

```
hello = "I am Lavinia, I am {}, I was born on the {}th and I weigh {} kg!"
print(hello.format(10, 24, 48))
```

Returns:

```
I am Lavinia, I am 10, I was born on the 24th and I weigh 48 kg!
```

Or associate these values with variables:

```
x, y, z = 10, 24, 48
hello = "I am Lavinia, I am {}, I was born on the {}th and I weigh {} kg!"
print(hello.format(x, y, z))
```

Returns:

```
I am Lavinia, I am 10, I was born on the 24th and I weigh 48 kg!
```

You can also insert numbers inside the braces that will refer to the values (or variables) of the **format()** function according to **indices** rules.

Example:

```
x, y, z = 50, 24, 48
hello = "I am Lavinia, I am {2}, I was born on the {1}th and I weigh {0} kg!"
print(ciao.format(x, y, z))
```

Returns:

```
I am Lavinia, I am 48, I was born on the 24th and I weigh 50 kg!
```

It's also possible to use so-called **named indexes**, assigning numerical values inside the
format() function. In the braces, we will refer to the variable names.

Example:

```
hello = "I am Lavinia, I am {x}, I was born on the {y}th and I weigh {z} kg!"
print(hello.format(x = 28, y = 24, z = 50))
```


Returns:

```
I am Lavinia, I am 28, I was born on the 24th and I weigh 50 kg!
```


Or, inside the **format()** function, we can still refer to variables.

Example:

```
years = 28
day = 24
weight = 50
hello = "I am Lavinia, I am {x}, I was born on the {y}th and I weigh {z} kg!"
print(hello.format(x = years, y = day, z = weight))
```


Returns:

```
I am Lavinia, I am 28, I was born on the 24th and I weigh 50 kg!
```


On the next page, there's a complete list of **string methods**.

REMEMBER:
*When a string delimited by single quotes contains one or more single quotes, or a string
delimited by double quotes contains one or more double quotes, you can use **escape characters**.
The symbol that would cause confusion (triggering the message* `SyntaxError: unterminated
string literal` *)
must be preceded by a backslash (\ ).*

E.g:

```
x = "They called me \"Know-it-all\" and I was very proud."

y = 'They called me \'Know-it-all\' and I was very proud.'
```

PYTHON STRING METHODS	
capitalize()	Converts the first character to upper case
casefold()	Converts string into lower case
center()	Returns a centered string
count()	Returns the number of times a specified value occurs in a string
encode()	Returns an encoded version of the string
endswith()	Returns true if the string ends with the specified value
expandtabs()	Sets the tab size of the string
find()	Returns the position of a specified value
format()	Formats specified values in a string
format_map()	Formats specified values in a string
index()	Returns the position of a specified value
isalnum()	Returns True if all characters in the string are alphanumeric
isalpha()	Returns True if all characters in the string are in the alphabet
isascii()	Returns True if all characters in the string are ascii characters
isdecimal()	Returns True if all characters in the string are decimals
isdigit()	Returns True if all characters in the string are digits
isidentifier()	Returns True if the string is an identifier
islower()	Returns True if all characters in the string are lower case
isnumeric()	Returns True if all characters in the string are numeric
isprintable()	Returns True if all characters in the string are printable
isspace()	Returns True if all characters in the string are whitespaces
istitle()	Returns True if the string follows the rules of a title
isupper()	Returns True if all characters in the string are upper case
join()	Converts the elements of an iterable into a string
ljust()	Returns a left justified version of the string
lower()	Converts a string into lower case
lstrip()	Returns a left trim version of the string
maketrans()	Returns a translation table to be used in translations
partition()	Returns a tuple where the string is parted into three parts
replace()	Replaces a specified value with a specified value
rfind()	Returns the position of a specified value
rindex()	Returns the position of a specified value
rjust()	Returns a right justified version of the string
rpartition()	Returns a tuple where the string is parted into three parts
rsplit()	Splits the string at the specified separator and returns a list
rstrip()	Returns a right trim version of the string
split()	Splits the string at the specified separator and returns a list
splitlines()	Splits the string at line breaks and returns a list
startswith()	Returns true if the string starts with the specified value
strip()	Returns a trimmed version of the string
swapcase()	Swaps cases, lower case becomes upper case and vice versa
title()	Converts the first character of each word to upper case
translate()	Returns a translated string
upper()	Converts a string into upper case
zfill()	Fills the string with a specified number of 0 values at the beginning

BOOLEAN: TRUE AND FALSE

The values **True** and **False** are crucial if we want to set up sequences of instructions whose execution or repetition depends on the truth or falsehood of a condition (*if* statement, *while* loop, etc.).

The **bool()** function converts a value into a boolean (True or False).

```
print(bool(1))
```
Returns True.

```
print(bool(0))
```
Returns False.

There are 7 values that return False:

- False
- None
- 0
- "" empty string
- [ ] empty list
- {} empty tuple
- () empty set

Even just printing something true or false generates the corresponding **boolean**:

```
print(5 < 3)
```
Returns False.

```
Print(5 < 10)
```
Returns True.

Let's look at a very simple example (we'll see the if statement in the following pages):

```
if 5 < 10:
    print("i'm less than 10")
else:
    print("i'm greater than 10")
```

In this example, the first line generates **True** or **False** and affects the printed statement.

Let's see another example:

```
wine = 0
if wine is True:
    print("pour a glass of wine")
else:
    print("we're out of wine")
```

In this example, the first line not only assigns a numerical value to the variable *wine* but also generates a **boolean** because 0 returns **False** (see previous page) and affects the printed statement.

A BIT OF MATHEMATICS

OPERATORS

Operators are symbols or keywords that perform mathematical, comparison, assignment, and logical operations on values. They are used to manipulate data within the code and control the program's execution flow.

The following table includes::

- Arithmetic operators: perform mathematical operations such as addition, subtraction, multiplication, and division.

- Comparison operators: perform comparisons between values, such as equal to, not equal to, greater than, less than, greater than or equal to, and less than or equal to.

- Assignment operators: assign values to variables, such as =, +=, -=, *=, and /=.

- Logical operators: perform logical operations, such as AND, OR, and NOT

- Membership operators: check if a value is present in a sequence, such as IN and NOT IN.

Each type of operator has its specific syntax and function.

TABLE OF OPERATORS		
OPERATOR	NAME	EXAMPLE
ARITHMETIC OPERATORS		
+	Addition	a + b
-	Subtraction	a - b
*	Multiplication	a * b
/	Division	a / b
%	Modulus	a % b
//	Floor Division	a // b
**	Exponentiation	a ** b
COMPARISON OPERATORS		
==	Equal to	a == b
!=	Not equal to	a != b
>	Greater than	a > b
<	Less than	a < b
>=	Greater than or equal to	a >= b
<=	Less than or equal to	a <= b
ASSIGNMENT OPERATORS		
=	Equal	a = b
+=	Addition and Assignment	a += 2 (a = a + 2)
-=	Subtraction and Assignment	a -= 2 (a = a - 2)
*=	Multiplication and Assignment	a *= 2 (a = a * 2)
/=	Division and Assignment	a /= 2 (a = a / 2)
%=	Modulus and Assignment	a %= 2 (a = a % 2)
//=	Floor Division and Assignment	a //= 2 (a = a // 2)
**=	Exponentiation and Assignment	a **= 2 (a = a ** 2)
LOGICAL OPERATORS		
and	True if both are true	a = 5 and b = 5
or	True if either is true	a = 5 or b = 5
not	Invert the result	not(a = 5)
MEMBERSHIP OPERATORS		
in	Present in string, list, etc.	if "apple" in fruit
not in	Not present	if "apple" not in fruit
IDENTITY OPERATORS		
is	Check an object	if x is True
is not	Invert the result	if x is not True

Here are some considerations about **arithmetic operators**:

- The **Modulus** operator returns the remainder of a division.

    Example:

    ```
    7.5 % 2 = 1.5
    ```

    (Result of division: 2, remainder: 1.5).

- The **Floor Division** operator, also known as **Integer Division**, divides the first number by the second and returns the result rounded down to the nearest integer.

    Example:

    ```
    15 // 4 = 3
    ```

    (While 15 / 4 = 3.75).

- When evaluating expressions, Python follows the operator precedence rules (first multiplication and division, then addition and subtraction). It also supports the use of parentheses to explicitly control the order of operations. This allows you to create complex expressions with clear precedence rules..

REMEMBER:
To determine whether a number is even or odd, you can use the modulus *arithmetic operator (%), which returns the remainder of a division.*

Example: `5 % 2`
   If there is no remainder, 5 is even. If there is a remainder, 5 is odd.

Similarly, you can determine if a number is divisible by another.

Example: `n % 3`
Let's assume n = 18. *If there is no remainder, 18 is divisible by 3.*

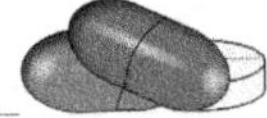

Some considerations about **assignment operators**:

To change the value of a variable, you can use two types of syntax.

An extended syntax:

```
x = 5
x = x + 2
```

And a shorter one:

```
x = 5
x += 2
```

In both cases **x** will have the value of 7.

The shorter syntax is valid for all the arithmetic operators we have seen in the table.

DID YOU KNOW?

*The **print()** function, by default, ends by adding a new line. With the **end** parameter, we can continue the line with the next **print**.*

Ex:

```
print("Midway upon the journey", end=" ")
print("of our life")
```

It will result in a single line:

```
Midway upon the journey of our life
```

BASIC MATHEMATICAL FUNCTIONS

The **abs()** function returns the absolute value of a number.

Example:

```
x = abs(-5)
```
x will be 5.

The **round()** function rounds a floating-point number.

Example:

```
x = round(5.4)
```
x will be 5.

The **pow()** function returns the power of a number.

Example:

```
x = pow(2,3)
```
x will be 8.

The **int()** function converts a string to an integer.

Example:

```
x = int("5")
```
x will be 5.

The **float()** function returns a floating-point number from a number or string.

Example:

```
x = float("5")
```
x will be 5.0.

The **min()** function returns the smallest value.

Example:

```
x = min(5, 10, 15)
```
x will be 5.

The **max()** function returns the largest value.

Example:

```
x = max(5, 10, 15)
```
x will be 15.

The **sum()** function adds the elements of a list.

Example:

```
numbers = [5, 10, 15]
x = sum(numbers)
```
x will be *30*.

To perform more complex mathematics, you will need to import the **math** module with the syntax.

```
import math
```

and call its functions using the syntax.

```
math.function
```

Example:

```
import math
x = math.sqrt(64)
```
x will be *8.0*.

For a comprehensive list of all **math** functions:

```
print(dir(math)
```

REMEMBER?

*The **help()** function provides information about a given instruction, module, class, function, etc. Its syntax is very simple:*

```
help(print)
```
> *displays documentation for the print() function,*

```
help(str)
```
> *displays documentation for the str() function.*

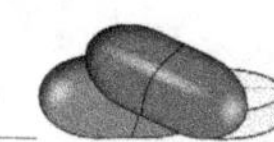

CONDITIONAL STATEMENTS

IF – ELIF – ELSE

The **IF – ELIF – ELSE** construct executes different instructions based on the occurrence of one or more conditions.

The simplest form is:

`if condition:`

executes a block of code only if the condition is true.

By adding

`else:`

Specifies a block of code to execute when the condition is false.

By adding one or more

`elif:`

Specifies other conditions.

Example 1 (*if, elif, else*):

```
x = 8
if x < 10:
    print("less than 10")
elif x == 10:
    print("equal to 10")
else:
    print("greater than 10")
```

Returns:

```
less than 10
```

Of course you can anticipate multiple scenarios.

Example:

____

```
if condition1:


elif condition2:


elif condition3:


else:
```

____

```
In this case:
```

- If *condition 1* is true it executes the corresponding code,
- <u>or</u> it proceeds to *condition 2*,
- <u>or</u> it proceeds to *condition 3*,
- <u>or</u> it proceeds to **else**.

Note that **only the code of the first <u>true</u> condition will be executed.** If none of the three conditions is true, the code associated with **else** will be executed.

INDENTATION

To hierarchically distinguish different parts of the code, we use **indentation**, which is a 4-space offset that establishes various levels and is crucial in IF, ELIF, and ELSE statements.

Let's further develop the example mentioned a few pages back:

```
x = 6
if x < 10:
    print("less than 10")
else:
    print("greater than 10")
```

Notice the use of indentation, which lowers the level of both **print()** statements, while both **if** and **else** are at the higher level.

Now let's see:

```
if condition1:
    print("condition1 is true")
    if condition2:
        print("condition1 is true, condition2 is true")
    else:
        print("condition1 is true, condition2 is false")
```

In this example, the **else statement** has the same level of indentation as the second **if** and is therefore executed when *condition1* is true and *condition2* is false. It would be different if the **else** had the same level of indentation as <u>the first if</u>: it would execute the associated code only if *condition1* were false.

In this case, we are talking about **nested if statements**, which we will see on the following page.

When you reduce the indentation, the loop or cycle ends.

NESTED IF STATEMENTS

Nested **if** statements are <u>conditional instructions</u> placed inside other **if** statements. They prove to be particularly useful for handling various shades of events or conditions.

In this simple example, as we have already seen, we pass the variable **x** through 2 filters: it can either be simply even or even and less than 10. If neither of these two conditions is met (**else**), another statement will be executed.

```
x = 2
if x % 2 == 0:
    print("Is even")
    if x < 10:
        print("Is even and less than 10")
else:
    print("Is odd")
```

Now let's look at something more structured by introducing the **input()** function, which takes input from the keyboard and returns it as a string. You will also use the **int()** function, which we have already seen, and it will allow you to perform simple checks on *n*.

In the following example, users will be prompted to enter a number. As mentioned, **input()** will assign that number to the variable *n* as a string, and **int()** will convert it into a number.

The variable will be passed through various filters to determine whether the number it contains is negative or positive and, in the latter case, whether it is greater than 100.

```
n = int(input("Enter a number:"))
if n >= 0:
    print("Equal to or greater than 0.")
    if n > 100:
        print("And also greater than 100.")
else:
    print("It's negative.")
```

Adding an **else** to the second **if** allows us to display a message if *n* is not greater than 100.

```
n = int(input("Enter a number:"))
if n >= 0:
    print("Equal to or greater than 0.")
    if n > 100:
        print("And also greater than 100.")
    else:
        print(“But it's not greater than 100.”)
else:
    print("It's negative.")
```

Alternatively, with a properly indented **if**, **elif**, **else** block, we can add more information if the entered number is negative.

```
n = int(input("Enter a number:"))
if n >= 0:
    print("Equal to or greater than 0.")
    if n > 100:
        print("And also greater than 100 .")
    else:
        print(“But it's not greater than 100 .”)
else:
    print("It's negative.")
    if n < -100:
        print(“And it's less than -100.”)
    elif n==-100:
        print(“And it's equal to -100.”)
    else:
        print(“And it's greater than -100.”)
```

LOOPS

A **loop** is a structure that repeatedly executes a block of instructions until specified conditions are met. The most common types of loops are **WHILE** and **FOR** loops.

WHILE

The **while** loop allows you to execute a series of instructions as long as the specified condition is true.

Let's examine a very simple loop that will run as long as *i* is less than 6:

```
i = 0
while i < 6:
    print(i)
    i += 1
```

In the first line, we set the variable **i**, the centerpiece of the loop, to a value of 0.

In the second line, we specify that the statement (the **print** function) will be executed as long as **i** is less than 6, which means for the cases 0, 1, 2, 3, 4, and 5..

In the fourth line, we need to increment **i** by one to keep track of the iterations.

The result of this very simple loop will be:

```
0
1
2
3
4
5
```

When you decrease the level of indentation, the **while** loop comes to an end..

I DO IT MYSELF:
To clear the screen, you can use the syntax:
```
import os
os.system("cls")
```

BREAK

The **break** statement is used to prematurely terminate a loop. In the following example, we see it, associated with an **if** statement, interrupting the loop when it reaches - or rather, exceeds - the number 3, unlike what the **while** loop would normally do:

```
i = 0
while i < 6:
    print(i)
    i += 1
    if i > 3:
        print("Early exit.")
        break
```

The screen output will be:

RANGE

The **range()** function, associated with a **for** loop, allows you to set a range of execution without using a string or a list but simply to execute the loop a certain number of times.

It's important to note that the counter will include the number 0 but stop just before the given number: **range(6)** returns values from 0 to 5.

```
for x in range(6):
    print(x)
```

Returns:

CONTINUE

The **continue** statement does not terminate the loop but rather skips a specific block of code and goes to the beginning of the loop.

Example:

```python
i = 0
while i < 6:
    i += 1
    if i == 3:
        print("Skipping the 3.")
        continue
    print(i)
```

We can notice a few things:

- When *i* is equal to 3, the program returns to the beginning of the **while** loop, so 3 will not be printed, but the loop will continue with the other numbers.

- The **continue** statement would not have made sense if the **print** statement had been placed immediately after the **while** loop, as in the previous examples, because returning to the beginning of the loop would not have prevented its execution. For this reason, it has been moved to the end.

- Note that reversing the order between `print(i)` and `i += 1` shifts the loop's cases from the range 0 - 5 to the range 1 - 6.

The screen output will be:

REMEMBER:
The equal operator *(==) must be distinguished from the simple equal symbol (=).*

   `x = 5` ⮕ *assigns the value 5 to x.*

   `if x == 5` ⮕ *if x is equal to 5.*

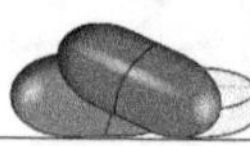

FOR

The **for** loop allows you to execute a series of instructions for all the elements in a *collection of data*, such as lists, tuples, sets... (Data collections will be covered in the following pages).

Let's see a simple example:

```
listCountries = [“California”, “Florida”, “Maine”]
for countries in listCountries:
    print(countries)
```

The screen output will be:

- In the first line, we assign a series of strings to *listCountries*.

- Nella seconda riga usiamo **for** seguito dalla variabile *nazioni* (avremmo potuto scegliere qualsiasi nome per la variabile), seguito da **in** e poi *listaNazioni*. Per ogni ciclo, la variabile *nazioni* assumerà il valore di una stringa presente in *listaNazioni*. Finite le stringhe il ciclo **for** termina.

- In the second line, we use **for** followed by the variable *countries* (we could have chosen any name for this variable), followed by **in**, and then *listCountries*. For each iteration, the variable *countries* will take on the value of a string present in *listCountries*. Whene there are no more strings, the **for** loop comes to an end.

- In the third line, the variable countries will be printed. As mentioned, it will change with each iteration.

Instead of a list, we can use a simple string, in which case there will be an iteration for each letter:

```
string = “apricot”
for letter in string:
    print(letter)
```

The screen output will be:

As long as there are letters in *string*, the **for** loop will print them one by one.

NESTED FOR LOOPS

Even **for** loops can be nested, either with each other or with **if** or **while** statements.

A small example of two nested **for** loops to display a 4 by 4 grid of numbers:

```
for x in range(3):
    for y in range(1, 5):
        print(y, end=" ")
    print()
```

Returns:

The outer loop (*x*) runs 4 times. Within it, the inner loop (*y*) also runs 4 times, but (since the **range** value will be printed) an interval of 1 to 5 is specified to obtain values 1, 2, 3, and 4.

In the third line, we print the value of *y*, taking care to use the **end** parameter to avoid a newline.

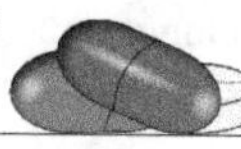

REMEMBER:
*In a **for** loop, the **break** and **continue** instructions can be used exactly as in a **while** loop.*

DATA COLLECTIONS

"We've already seen that variables are containers that can hold any type of information: numbers (5), strings ('hello'), booleans (True), etc...

To define containers that can hold a larger amount of information or entire data structures, we need to talk about **lists**, **tuples**, **sets**, and **dictionaries**.

- A **list** is an **ordered** collection of data. It's **modifiable** and allows **duplicates**[1]. Each element in the list is accessible by an index, and you can add, remove, or modify elements within it.

- A **tuple** is an **ordered** collection of data. It's **unmodifiable**. Allows **duplicates**. Once a tuple is created, you cannot change its content. It's often used for data that should not be modified.

- A **set** is an **unordered** collection of data. It's **unmodifiable**. **Does not** allow **duplicates**. Sets are useful for removing duplicates from a sequence of data and for performing set operations like union, intersection, difference, etc.

- A **dictionary** is an **unordered** collection of data that stores information in **key-value** pairs. It's **modifiable**. **Does not** allow **duplicates** in keys. Dictionaries are used to represent structured data where you need to access a value associated with a specific key.

Let's examine them in detail.

---

[1] When it's mentioned that a collection allows duplicates, it means that the collection can contain multiple elements with the same content. For example, in a list or a set, you may have multiple elements with the same value.

LISTS

ORDERED. INDEXED. MODIFIABLE. ALLOW DUPLICATES.

In order to create a **list**, we can use the **list()** constructor.

```
x = list(("hello", 37, True))
print(x)
```

Returns:

```
['hello', 37, True]
```

Alternatively, square brackets **[ ]**:

```
x = ["hello", 37, True]
print(x)
```

Returns:

```
['hello', 37, True]
```

Please note that **lists** can contain different data types: strings, numbers, booleans.

The **type()** function returns the data type of an object.

```
print(type(x))
```
Returns: `class 'list'`

The **len()** function returns the number of elements (length) in an object.

```
print(len(x))
```
Returns: `3`

ELEMENT POSITION

The **index()** method returns the position of an element.

- If there are multiple occurrences, it returns only the first one.

- If there are no occurrences, it returns an error message.

Example:

```
colors = ["red", "yellow", "green", "white", "black"]
print(colors.index("yellow"))
```

Returns: `1`

Remember that indexing starts from 0, not from 1, so the second element (yellow) will have position 1.

If we try to search for a non-existent element

```
colors = ["red", "yellow", "green", "white", "black"]
print(colors.index("blu"))
```

index() returns an error message:

```
Traceback (most recent call last):
File "", line 2, in <module>
print(colors.index("blu"))
ValueError: 'blu' is not in list
```

that we will handle by programming exceptions using **try** and **except**, which we will see later.

ACCESSING ELEMENTS

As we have seen with strings, we use the **slicing operator** (**[ ]**) to access elements in a **list**. The expression inside the brackets specifies the index of the element.

Example:

```
colors = ["red", "yellow", "green", "white", "black"]
print(colors[3])
```

Returns: `white`

Example with a negative index:

```
colors = ["red", "yellow", "green", "white", "black"]
print(colors[-1])
```

Returns: `black`

Remember that indices can also include ranges of values.

Example:

`[1:3]` = from 1 to 3, excluding 3.

```
colors = ["red", "yellow", "green", "white", "black"]
print(colors[1:3])
```

Returns: `'yellow', 'green'`

Example:

`[-3:-1]` = from -3 to -1, excluding -1.

```
colors = ["red", "yellow", "green", "white", "black"]
print(colors[-3:-1])
```

Returns: `'green', 'white'`

Example:

`[:3]` = from the beginning to 3, excluding 3.

```
colors = ["red", "yellow", "green", "white", "black"]
print(colors[:3])
```

Returns: `'red', 'yellow', 'green'`

Example:

`[2:]` = from 2 to the end.

```
colors = ["red", "yellow", "green", "white", "black"]
print(colors[2:])
```

Returns: `'green', 'white', 'black'`

REMEMBER:
*The **hash** symbol (#) placed at the beginning of a line allows you to insert comments in the code or disable portions that you currently don't need.*

MODIFYING ELEMENTS

The **slicing operator** ([ ]) can also be used to modify elements using the following syntax:

Example 1:

```
colors = ["red", "yellow", "green", "white", "black"]
colors[1] = "blu"
```

It replaces position 1, which is the string "yellow," with the new string "blue."

Example 2:

```
colors = ["red", "yellow", "green", "white", "black"]
colors[1:3] = "blu", "pink"
```

It replaces position 1, which is the string "yellow," with the new string "blue" and position 2, which is the string "green" with the new string "pink".

INSERTING ELEMENTS

There are various methods for inserting elements into a **list**, each with its own characteristics.

The **append()** method inserts the new element at the end of the list.

```
colors = [“red”, “yellow”, “green”, “white”, “black”]
colors.append(“blu”)
```

Returns: `'red', 'yellow', 'green', 'white', 'black', 'blu'`

The **insert()** method inserts the new element at a specific position.

```
colors = [“red”, “yellow”, “green”, “white”, “black”]
colors.insert(1, “blu”)
```

Returns: `'red', 'blu', 'yellow', 'green', 'white', 'black'`

DID YOU KNOW?

*To check if a specific string is present in a list, you can use the **in** operator. If you need to verify that a string is <u>not</u> present, you can use the **not in** operator.*

Example:

```
shapes = [“triangle”, “square”, “circle”]

if “triangle” in shapes: print (“It's there!”)
if “triangle” not in shapes: print (“It's not there!”)
```

The **extend()** method adds all the elements of an *iterable* (list, tuple, string, etc...) to the end of a **list**.

```
colors = ["red", "yellow", "green", "white", "black"]
shapes = ["triangle", "square", "circle"]
colors.extend(shapes)
```

In the example above, **extend()** adds the contents of the *shapes* list to the *colors* list.

It's important to note that the *shapes* list will remain exactly the same, while from now on, the *colors* list will be:

```
'red', 'yellow', 'green', 'white', 'black', 'triangle', 'square', 'circle'
```

The same result would be achieved using the + operator with the following syntax:

```
colors = colors + shapes
```

REMOVING ELEMENTS

There are various methods to remove elements from a list.

The **remove()** method removes the specified element.

```
colors = ["red", "yellow", "green", "white", "black"]
colors.remove("green")
```

Returns: `'red', 'yellow', 'white', 'black'`

The **pop()** method removes the element located at a given index..

```
colors = ["red", "yellow", "green", "white", "black"]
colors.pop(2)
```

Returns: `'red', 'yellow', 'white', 'black'`

If you don't provide any index within the parentheses, **pop()** removes the last element.

```
colors = ["red", "yellow", "green", "white", "black"]
colors.pop()
```

Returns: `'red', 'yellow', 'green', 'white'`

The **clear()** method removes all the elements from a list.

```
colors = ["red", "yellow", "green", "white", "black"]
colors.clear()
```

The *colors* list still exists but will be empty.

The **del** command completely removes an object, such as a variable, a list, or any element. For this reason, it can be used <u>with an index</u> to delete a single string from a list or <u>without an index</u> to delete the list itself.

Example of **del** with an index:

```
colors = ["red", "yellow", "green", "white", "black"]
del colors[2]
```

Returns: `'red', 'yellow', 'white', 'black'`

Example of **del** without an index:

```
colors = ["red", "yellow", "green", "white", "black"]
del colors
```

The *colors* list no longer exists.

UNPACKING LISTS

It is possible to extract all the elements from a **list** and assign each of them to a variable.

Example:

```
colors = [“red”, “yellow”, “green”]
(x, y, z) = colors
```

The variable x will contain the string "red", y will contain the string "yellow" and z will contain the string "green".

The number of variables must be equal to the number of elements in the **list**; otherwise, an error occurs. However, if the number of elements is greater than the number of variables, you can prefix an asterisk (*) before the last variable. This variable will become a list itself, and all the remaining elements will be assigned to it.

```
colors = [“red”, “yellow”, “green”, “white”, “black”]
(x, y, *z) = colors
```

The variable x will contain the string "red", y will contain the string "yellow" and z will be a new **list**, and its content will be: `['green', 'white', 'black']`

I DO IT MYSELF:
*You can check with a single line whether a specific element is present in a **list** using the syntax:*

```
print(“element” in list)
```

The result will simply be: `True` *or* `False`

CYCLING THROUGH ELEMENTS

Now let's see how to iterate through the elements of lists, referring to what we've covered in the chapter on loops.

The following examples display all the elements of the *colors* list.

A **for** loop:

```
colors = ["red", "yellow", "green", "white", "black"]
for element in colors:
    print(element)
```

Another **for** loop but, this time,

- in line 2, we use **range()** and **len()** to determine the number of iterations equal to the number of elements in the list and

- in line 3, we display the *colors* list taken at the index given by the variable *i*.

```
colors = ["red", "yellow", "green", "white", "black"]
for i in range(len(colors)):
    print(colors[i])
```

A **while** loop:

```
colors = ["red", "yellow", "green", "white", "black"]
i = 0
while i < len(colors):
    print(colors[i])
    i += 1
```

MODIFYING AND COPYING LISTS

The **sort()** method arranges the elements of the list in alphabetical order or from smallest to largest in the case of numbers.

Example:

```
colors = ["red", "yellow", "green", "white", "black"]
colors.sort()
```

Returns: `'black', 'green', 'red', 'white', 'yellow'`

For reverse order:

```
colors = ["red", "yellow", "green", "white", "black"]
colors.sort(reverse = True)
```

Returns: `'yellow', 'white', 'red', 'green', 'black'`

The **copy()** and **list()** methods create a copy of the list.

Example:

```
a = b.copy()
```

```
a = list(b)
```

Both examples create a list *a* that is a copy of the existing list *b*.

It's important to note that the syntax

```
a = b
```

also creates a copy, but in doing so, you would have two identical, linked lists: if one of them is modified, the other will undergo the same changes.

COMBINING THE LISTS

It's possible to merge two lists using the simple syntax

```
listA = listB + listC
```

But there are also other ways.

Using a **for()** loop and **append()**:

```
colors = ["red", "yellow", "green", "white", "black"]
shapes = ["triangle", "square", "circle"]
for element in shapes:
    colors.append(element)
```

You will get a loop with 3 iterations in which **append()** will add an element from the *shapes* list to the end of the *colors* list each time.

The *colors* list will become:

```
'red', 'yellow', 'green', 'white', 'black', 'triangle', 'square', 'circle'
```

The **extend()** method adds all the elements of one list to another list.

```
colors = ["red", "yellow", "green", "white", "black"]
shapes = ["triangle", "square", "circle"]
colors.extend(shapes)
```

The *colors* list will become:

```
'red', 'yellow', 'green', 'white', 'black', 'triangle', 'square', 'circle'
```

LIST COMPREHENSION

Often, a list is composed of elements derived from other sequences that have undergone operations or satisfy certain conditions. **List comprehension** is an elegant way to construct lists based on existing lists.

Let's go back to iterating through the elements of the *colors* list with a simple **for** loop, and display all elements that are different from the string 'green' (using an **if** statement):

```
colors = ["red", "yellow", "green", "white", "black"]
for color in colors:
    if color != "green":
        print(color)
```

We have a list of elements based on the existing *colors* list.

Let's try to do the same thing in a single line of code instead of three:

```
colors = ["red", "yellow", "green", "white", "black"]
[print(color) for color in colors if color != "green"]
```

We achieved the same result by writing something like:

```
[print the variable color, for all elements in the colors list, as
long as it is different from the string "green"]
```

All in one line using a **list comprehension**.

Let's look at a series of examples that will clarify the concept better than many words.

We create the list *squares*, loop the variable *n* over a range of 6 (so from 0 to 5), and for each value of *n*, we add to the *squares* list the number obtained by squaring *n*.

```
squares = []
for n in range(6):
    squares.append(n**2)
print(squares)
```

Let's do the same thing using a **list comprehension**:

```
squares = [n**2 for n in range(6)]
print(squares)
```

Both of them return:

```
[0, 1, 4, 9, 16, 25]
```

Starting from the list *numbers*, we create the list *doubles*. We loop through the variable *n* for each element in *numbers*, and for each value of *n*, we add to the *doubles* list the number obtained by multiplying *n* by 2.

```
numbers = [3, 4, 5]
doubles = []
for n in numbers:
    doubles.append(n*2)
print(doubles)
```

Let's do the same thing using a **list comprehension**:

```
numbers = [3, 4, 5]
doubles = [n*2 for n in numbers]
print(doubles)
```

Both of them return:

```
[6, 8, 10]
```

Example with 2 **for** loops:

```python
coordinate = []
for x in range(3):
    for y in range(3):
        coordinate.append((x, y))
print(coordinate)
```

Let's do the same thing using a **list comprehension**:

```python
coordinate = [(x, y) for x in range(3) for y in range(3)]
print(coordinate)
```

Both of them return:

```
[(0, 0), (0, 1), (0, 2), (1, 0), (1, 1), (1, 2), (2, 0), (2, 1), (2, 2)]
```

Example with 2 **for** loops and an **if**:

```python
evenNumbers = []
for x in range(1, 4):
    for y in range(1, 5):
        if (x*y)%2 == 0:
            evenNumbers.append(x*y)
print(evenNumbers)
```

Let's do the same thing using a **list comprehension**:

```python
evenNumbers = [x*y for x in range(1, 4) for y in range(1, 5) if (x*y)%2 == 0]
print(evenNumbers)
```

Both of them return:

```
[2, 4, 2, 4, 6, 8, 6, 12]
```

TUPLES

ORDERED. INDEXED. UNMODIFIABLE. ALLOW DUPLICATES.

In order to create a **tuple**, we can use the **tuple()** constructor:

```
x = tuple(("hello", 37, True))
print(x)
```

Returns:

```
['hello', 37, True]
```

Alternatively, round brackets ( ):

```
x = ("hello", 37, True)
print(x)
```

Returns:

```
['hello', 37, True]
```

Note that **tuples** can contain different data types: string, number, boolean.

To create a **tuple** containing a single element, you need to add a comma, which distinguishes it from a regular string:

```
x = ("hello",)
```
is a **tuple** containing a single element.

```
x = ("hello")
```
is a string.

The **type()** and **len()** functions return the data type and the number of elements (length) of a **tuple**, just like with lists.

POSITION AND ACCESS TO ELEMENTS

Just like with **lists**, for **tuples**, we use the **index()** method or the **slice operator ([ ])** with the appropriate indices to access the elements.

MODIFY, INSERT, REMOVE ELEMENTS

Since **tuples** are immutable and are suitable for representing collections of data that never change, they cannot be subject to **append()**, **insert()**, **extend()**, **remove()** and **pop()**.

It is still possible to use the **del** command, which, as mentioned, completely removes an object, including a **tuple**.

There is, however, the possibility to convert the **tuple** into a list, apply our modifications, insertions, removals, etc., and then convert it back into the original **tuple**.

Example:

```
fruit = ("apple", "pear", "orange")
fruit2 = list(fruit)
fruit2[0] = "cherry"
fruit = tuple(fruit2)
```

- In line 1, we assign strings to the **tuple** *fruit*.

- In line 2, we use the **list()** constructor to create a list (*fruit2*) that is a copy of the *fruit* **tuple**.

- In line 3, we make our modifications, in this case: we replace the element "apple" with the new element "cherry".

- In line 4, we use the **tuple()** constructor to create a **tuple** (*fruit*) that is a copy of the list *fruit2* and will replace the old version.

The *fruit* **tuple** has been successfully modified!

To concatenate **tuples**, you can use the **+** operator.

UNPACKING TUPLES

To retrieve all the elements of a **tuple** and assign each of them to a variable, you do it in the same way as with lists.

In this case, if the number of elements is greater than the number of variables, you can put an asterisk (*) before the last variable. It will then become a **list** (note: not a **tuple**), and all the remaining elements will be assigned to it.

ITERATING THROUGH ELEMENTS

Regarding **loops**, there is no difference between **tuples** and **lists**.

REMEMBER:
*The **count()** and **index()** methods have the same syntax. The first one returns the number of occurrences for an element in a **list** or a **tuple**, while the second one returns the position at which the specified element is located.*

Example:

```
fruit = ("apple", "pear", "orange", "pear")
print(fruit.index("pear")
print(fruit.count("pear")
```

The second line will return the position of "pear": **1**
The third line will return how many times "pear" appears: **2**

SETS

UNORDERED. UNINDEXED. UNMODIFIABLE. NO DUPLICATES.

In order to create a **set**, we can use the **set()** constructor:

```
x = set(("hello", 37, True))
print(x)
```

Returns:

`['hello', 37, True]` in any order.

Or curly braces { }:

```
x = {"hello", 37, True}
print(x)
```

Returns:

`['hello', 37, True]` in any order.

Note that **sets** can contain different data types: string, number, boolean.

The **type()** and **len()** functions return the data type and the number of elements (length) of a **set**, just like with lists.

POSITION AND ACCESS TO ELEMENTS

To access individual elements, since **sets** are unordered, we can use, for example, a **for** loop:

```
animals = {"dog", "cat", "hamster"}
for element in animals:
    print(element)
```

In this example, we will display all the strings from the **set** *animals,* but never in the same order.

INSERT OR REMOVE ELEMENTS

The **add()** method adds an element to a **set**, and if the element already exists, **add()** does not add anything.

```
animals = {"dog", "cat", "hamster"}
animals.add("hawk")
```

The **remove()** method removes the specified element.

The **discard()** method also removes an element from a **set**. However, while the **remove()** method raises an error if the specified element doesn't exist, the **discard()** method does not raise any errors.

The **pop()** method removes a random element. When used with **sets**, specifying an index within parentheses will generate an error.

The **clear()** method removes all elements from the **set**.

The **del** command, as seen earlier, removes any object, including a **set**.

MERGING SETS, ISOLATING, AND REMOVING DUPLICATES

The **union()** method returns a new **set** containing the elements from the original **set** and those from the **set** passed as an argument, removing duplicates.

```
animals = {"dog", "cat", "hamster", "rabbit"}
otherAnimals = {"rabbit", "parrot", "dog"}
newAnimals = animals.union(otherAnimals)
print(newAnimals)
```

Returns:

`['dog', 'hamster', 'parrot', 'cat', 'rabbit']` in any order.

The **update()** method adds the elements from another **set** (passed as an argument) to the current **set**.

```
animals = {"dog", "cat", "hamster", "rabbit"}
otherAnimals = {"rabbit", "parrot", "dog"}
animals.update(otherAnimals)
print(animals)
```

Returns:

`['dog', 'hamster', 'parrot', 'cat', 'rabbit']` in any order.

NOTE: Both **union()** and **update()** will include any duplicates <u>only once</u>.

The **intersection()** method returns a new **set** that contains only the duplicated elements among the elements of the original **set** and the **set** passed as an argument.

```
animals = {"dog", "cat", "hamster", "rabbit"}
otherAnimals = {"rabbit", "parrot", "dog"}
newAnimals = animals.intersection(otherAnimals)
print(newAnimals)
```

Returns:

`['dog', 'rabbit']` in any order.

The **intersection_update()** method retains in the **set** only the elements that are common with another **set** (passed as an argument).

```
animals = {"dog", "cat", "hamster", "rabbit"}
otherAnimals = {"rabbit", "parrot", "dog"}
animals.intersection_update(otherAnimals)
print(animals)
```

Returns:

`['dog', 'rabbit']` in any order.

DID YOU KNOW?

*An **f-string** inside a* print *function is a string literal that contains expressions within curly braces. Instead of the expressions, the corresponding values will be displayed on the screen. Example:*

```
x = "Mark"
y = 42
print(f"My name is {x} and I'm {y} years old.")
```

Returns:

`My name is Mark and I'm 42 years old.`

The **symmetric_difference()** method returns a new **set** that contains the elements from the original **set** and those from the **set** passed as an argument, excluding the duplicated elements.

```
animals = {"dog", "cat", "hamster", "rabbit"}
otherAnimals = {"rabbit", "parrot", "dog"}
newAnimals = animals.symmetric_difference(otherAnimals)
print(newAnimals)
```

Returns:

`['cat', 'parrot', 'hamster']` in any order.

The **symmetric_difference_update()** method adds the elements from another **set** (passed as an argument) to the current **set**, excluding any duplicate elements.

```
animals = {"dog", "cat", "hamster", "rabbit"}
otherAnimals = {"rabbit", "parrot", "dog"}
animals.symmetric_difference_update(otherAnimals)
print(animals)
```

Returns:

`['cat', 'parrot', 'hamster']` in any order.

DICTIONARIES

ORDERED. MODIFIABLE. NO DUPLICATES.

Dictionaries are used to store data in <u>key/value pairs</u>.

In order to create a **dictionary**, we can use the **dict()** constructor:

```
student = dict([("Name", "Mark")])
print(student)
```

Returns:

```
{'Name': 'Mark'}
```

Or curly braces { }:

```
student = {"Name" : "Mark",
           "Surname" : "Rogers",
           "Age" : 25}
print(student)
```

Returns:

```
{'Name' : 'Mark', 'Surname' : 'Rogers', 'Age' : 25}
```

The **dictionary** can also be written in a single line; if you use automatic indentation, it will format the data as shown above.

Note that **dictionaries** can contain different data types: string, number, boolean.

The **type()** and **len()** functions return the data type and the number of elements (key/value pairs) of a **set**, just like with lists.

ACCESS TO ELEMENTS

The **get()** method returns the value of the specified key.

```
print(student.get("Name"))
```
Returns: `Mark`

You can access the value of a key using the **subscript operator ([ ])** as well.

```
print(student["Name"]
```
Returns: `Mark`

The **keys()** method returns the list of keys.

```
print(student.keys())
```
Returns: `dict keys(['Name', 'Surname', 'Age'])`

The **values()** method returns the list of values.

```
print(student.values())
```
Returns: `dict values(['Mark', 'Rogers', 25])`

The **items()** method returns a list of tuples (key, value).

```
print(student.items())
```
Returns: `dict items([('Name', 'Mark'), ('Surname', 'Rogers'), ('Age', 25)])`

> **DID YOU KNOW?**
> *You can check if a specific key exists in a **dictionary** with a single line of code using the syntax:*
>
> ```
> print("key" in dictionary)
> ```
>
> *The result will simply be:* `True` *or* `False`

MODIFY, ADD, REMOVE ELEMENTS

The **update()** method modifies the value of a specified key.

```
student.update({"Name" : "Anna"})
```

Associates the value *Anna* with the key *Name*, replacing the value *Mark*.

If the key does not exist, a new key/value pair is added to the **dictionary**.

```
student.update({"Course" : "Biology"})
```

Adds the key / value pair *Course : Biology*.

The same thing can be done using square brackets [ ].

```
student["Name"] = "Anna"
```

Associates the value *Anna* with the key *Name*, replacing the value *Mark*.

If the key does not exist, a new key/value pair is added to the **dictionary**.

```
student["Course"] = "Biology"
```

Adds the key / value pair *Course : Biology*.

The **pop()** method removes the specified key / value pair.

```
student.pop("Name")
```

Deletes the key *Name* and its value.

The **popitem()** method removes the last key / value pair.

```
student.popitem()
```

Deletes the key / value pair *Age : 25*.

The **clear()** method removes all elements from the **dictionary**.

```
student.clear()
```

Completely empty the *student* **dictionary**.

The **del** statement can be used <u>with a key</u> to delete a <u>key / value pair</u>.

```
del student["Name"]
```

Delete the key *Name* and its value.

To completely delete the **dictionary** using the **del** command, you can use the following syntax:

```
del student
```

Completely deletes the *student* **dictionary**.

DID YOU KNOW?

*The **pass** statement is a <u>null</u> statement . It is used when a statement is required, but we do not want any code to be executed.*

```
def name_function():
    pass
```

```
for i in range(10):
    pass
```

It is useful when you are working on code and haven't yet decided what you want to happen in a specific function or loop, but you don't want to generate an error.

CYCLING THROUGH ELEMENTS

Using a **for** loop and some of the methods seen so far, we can access **dictionaries** in various ways.

Let's see some examples:

```
for x in student:
    print(x)
```

Returns the list of *keys*.

```
for x in student:
    print(student[x])
```

Returns the list of *values*.

```
for x in student.keys():
    print(x)
```

Returns the list of *keys*.

```
for x in student.values():
    print(x)
```

Returns the list of *values*.

```
for x, y in student.items():
    print(x, y)
```

Returns a list of tuples (key, value).

COPYING DICTIONARIES

Both the **copy()** method and the **dict()** constructor create a copy of the **dictionary**.

```
a = b.copy()
```

```
a = dict(b)
```

Both examples create a list *a* that is a copy of the existing list *b*.

Once again, we note that the syntax

```
a = b
```

creates a copy, but in doing so, you would have two identical, linked lists: if one is modified, the other will undergo the same changes.

NESTED DICTIONARIES

Nested **dictionaries** are **dictionaries** within other **dictionaries**.

Example:

```
student = {"Name" : "Mark",
           "Surname" : "Rogers",
           "Age" : 25,
           "Address" : {
               "City" : "Rome",
               "Street" : "Church",
               "Number" : 33}}
```

To access the *Address* **dictionary**, we use square brackets:

```
print(student["Address"])
```

Returns: `{'City': 'Rome', 'Street': 'Church', 'Number': 33}`

To go down one level and access a single element of the *Address* **dictionary**, we specify the underlying key:

```
print(student["Address"]["Number"])
```

Returns: `33`

With the same logic, we can **add**, **remove**, or **modify** elements in each nested **dictionary**.

FUNCTIONS

Functions are a tool that allows us to group a set of instructions that perform a specific task. They take input arguments (although there can be **functions** without arguments), process them, and return a result as output.

Once a function is defined, you can execute it (*call it*) whenever you need it, potentially passing different arguments depending on the situation. This results in more streamlined and organized code, avoiding unnecessary repetitions.

Let's clarify the concept of a **function** by taking simple everyday actions as examples.

To define a function:

```
def wear_clothes():
    print("Put on pants.")
    print("Put on a shirt.")
    print("Put on shoes.")
```

Call the function:

```
wear_clothes()
```

Every time we *call* the function, the following will appear on the screen:

```
Put on pants.
Put on a shirt.
Put on shoes.
```

DID YOU KNOW?
Using triple single quotes (''') or triple double quotes (""") *you can create a comment line that identifies the **function**.*

E.g.:

```
def wear_clothes()
    '''sequence of clothing to wear'''
```

*It will be particularly useful in the case of more complex **functions**.*

PARAMETERS

Depending on the occasions, we might want to choose whether to wear sneakers or slippers. Let's add some **parameters**:

```
def wear_clothes (type_of_footwear):
    print("Put on pants.")
    print("Put on a shirt.")
    print("Put on " + type_of_footwear + ".")

wear_clothes("slippers")
```

The screen output will be:

```
Put on pants.
```

```
Put on a shirt.
```

```
Put on slippers.
```

- Note that the **parameter** *footwear_type* has been placed within the parentheses when defining the **function**,

- it has been specifically called in the fourth line of code,

- it was also invoked when the **function** itself has been *called*. We passed the <u>argument</u> *slippers* to it.

Let me give another example, this time with <u>two parameters</u>.

```
def wear_clothes (type_of_footwear, cap):
    print("Put on pants.")
    print("Put on a shirt.")
    print("Put on " + type_of_footwear + ".")
    if cap:
        print("Put on the cap.")

wear_clothes ("sneakers", True)
```

The screen output will be:

```
Put on pants.
```

```
Put on a shirt.
```

```
Put on slippers.
```

```
Put on the cap.
```

The second **parameter**, *cap*, will be a *boolean*.

This is because, inside the **function**, we reference it with the line: `if cap:`, which means that if we pass **True** to *cap* when *calling* the function, it will display the phrase *"Put on the cap"*. If we pass *False*, nothing will happen.

Actually, any non-empty string will be interpreted as *True*, while an empty string will return *False* (see page 15). You could call the function with the syntax:

```
wear_clothes("sneakers", "hello")
```

and you would still achieve the same result.

DID YOU KNOW?

You can use an infinite loop (`while True`) to stay inside a function or to prevent a program from ending until the user decides to do so.

Example:

```
while True:
    user_choice = input("Do you want to continue? (Yes/No) ")
    if user_choice.lower() == "no":
        break
    print("The program is still running.")
```

ARBITRARY ARGUMENTS

Instead of a defined number of parameters, we can use a single generic name preceded by an asterisk (*), which in this case is not just the simple arithmetic operator but is called the **unpacking operator**.

Of course, to access the arguments inside the function, we will need to use indices within square brackets.

Let's take a closer look by rewriting the last example:

```
def wear_clothes(*arguments):
    print("Put on pants.")
    print("Put on a shirt.")
    print("Put on " + arguments[0] + ".")
    if arguments[1]:
        print("Put on the cap.")

wear_clothes("sneakers", True)
```

The screen output will be:

```
Put on pants.
Put on a shirt.
Put on sneakers.
Put on the cap.
```

Please note that:

- in the first line of code, we left the number of parameters undefined by writing ***arguments**,

- in the fourth line, we used an index *(arguments[0])*,

- in the fifth line, we used an index *(arguments[1])*,

- when *calling* the function, we assigned a string and a boolean (*sneakers* and *True*) to ***arguments**.

KEYWORD ARGUMENTS

Calling a **function** with **parameters**, as we've seen so far, without passing any arguments will result in an error. To avoid this, we use **keyword arguments**, which are parameters that already have default values.

The syntax is *parameter = argument*

Let's rewrite the same example once more:

```
def wear_clothes(type_of_footwear = "sneakers", cap = True):
    print("Put on pants.")
    print("Put on a shirt.")
    print("Put on " + type_of_footwear + ".")
    if cap:
        print("Put on the cap.")

wear_clothes()
```

As you can see, the **function** is called without passing any arguments. In this case, it will return the default arguments (*sneakers* and *True*), and

the screen output will be:

```
Put on pants.
Put on a shirt.
Put on sneakers.
Put on the cap.
```

Calling the **function** with arguments,

```
wear_clothes("slippers", False)
```

the screen output will be:

```
Put on pants.
Put on a shirt.
Put on slippers.
```

THE SCOPE AND THE RETURN FUNCTION

Scope refers to the region of the program where a variable is available.

Variables declared within a function are called **local** and are not available outside of it, while those declared outside a function are called **global** and are accessible throughout the program.

The **return** function allows passing the value of a variable from **local** to **global**.

Example:

```
def power_to(n1, n2):
    '''n1 is the base, n2 is the exponent'''
    power = n1 ** n2
    return power

x = power_to(2, 3)

print(x)
```

The screen output will be: 8

Without the `return power` line,

the screen output will be: None

because the **function** performs the task it was written for but does not return the value of *power*.

It is possible to assign a value to a **local** variable within a function even if there is already a **global** variable with a different value. Inside the function (and in all nested functions), the **local** variable will have the value, but once you exit the function, the **global** variable will have the value.

To indicate that a variable is **global**, even from within a function, you need to use the **global** keyword.

Example:

```
x = 10

def change_x():
    global x
    x = 20

print("Before calling the function, x is", x)

change_x()

print("After calling the function, x is", x)
```

The screen output will be:

```
Before calling the function, x is 10
After calling the function, x is 20
```

CLASSES AND OBJECTS

Object-oriented programming (OOP) is a programming method that uses **classes** and **objects** to represent data and behavior. The code is organized around **objects**, which contain data and methods instead of variables and functions.

A **class** defines the structure of an **object** and its behavior. An **object** is an instance of a class, a realization of it.

Let's take it step by step.

```python
class Student:

    name = "Mark"
    surname = "Rogers"

student1 = Student()
student2 = Student()

print(student1)
print(student2)
```

In this example:

- in the first line, you create the **class** *Student* (it's a good practice to write the name of a class with a capital letter),

- in lines 2 and 3, you define properties or attributes: *name* and *surname*,

- in lines 4 and 5, you create **objects** - instances of the **class**,

- in lines 6 and 7, you display the two **objects**.

The screen output will be:

```
main   .Student object at 0x0000…
main   .Student object at 0x0000…
```

That is, two **objects** of the *Student* **class** and the memory allocation in which they reside.

Both objects have a *first name* and a *last name*, but they are both named Mark Rogers. Let's see how, with the help of the **constructor**, you can create infinitely many objects, all different from each other.

THE CONSTRUCTOR AND OTHER METHODS

The **__init__** method, also known as the initializer or **constructor method**, defines the characteristics of the **object**. By convention, the first parameter passed to it is *self*, which ensures that the attributes - or properties - will be associated with the **instance-objects**.

The subsequent parameters will be the properties of each **object**, as follows:

```
def __init__(self, name, surname):
```

These will also be invoked in the subsequent lines:

```
self.name = name
self.surname = surname
```

Every time you want to create an **object** from this **class**, you will specify its attributes using the syntax:

```
student1 = Student(name, surname)
```

Let's take a closer look by rewriting the example just given:

```
class Student:

    def __init__(self, name, surname):
        self.name = name
        self.surname = surname

student1 = Student("Mark", "Rogers")
student2 = Student("Anna", "White")

print((student1.name), (student1.surname))
print((student2.name), (student2.surname))
```

This time,

- in line 2, you use the constructor **__init__**,

- which allows you, in lines 3 and 4, to define the attributes.

- In lines 5 and 6, you create **objects** by assigning them parameters.

- In lines 7 and 8, you display the attributes of both objects and see that they are different:

```
Mark Rogers
```

```
Anna White
```

Both objects have a *first name* and a *last name* but, thanks to the **constructor**, each one is different from the others.

Let's now rewrite the same example by adding two more **methods**.

The *greet* **method**, that will make the **object** perform a simple action.

The *attributes* **method** will display all the **object**'s properties.

```python
class Student:

    def __init__(self, name, surname):
        self.name = name
        self.surname = surname

    def greet(self):
        print(f"Hello! My name is {self.name}.")

    def attributes(self):
        print(f"Name: {self.name}")
        print(f"Surname: {self.surname}")


student1 = Student("Mark", "Rogers")


student1.greet()
student1.attributes()
```

The screen output will be:

```
Hello! My name is Mark.
Name: Mark
Surname: Rogers
```

MODIFY AND DELETE OBJECT PROPERTIES

Based on the previous example,

to modify any attribute of an **object**, we can use the syntax:

```
Student1.name = "Peter"
```

The screen output will be:

```
Hello! My name is Peter.
```

to <u>delete</u> any attribute of an **object**, you can use the **del** command, with the syntax:

```
del student1.name
```

to completely <u>delete</u> the **object** you can use the **del** command, with the syntax:

```
del student1
```

INHERITANCE

Inheritance is a concept that allows you to create a new class based on an existing class. The <u>derived class</u> (*child class*) inherits all the properties and methods of the <u>base class</u> (*parent class*) but can also modify or extend functionality.

Let's take a look at and discuss an example:

```python
class Person:
    def __init__(self, name, surname):
        self.name = name
        self.surname = surname

    def greet(self):
        print(f"Hello! My name is {self.name}")

class Teacher(Person):
    pass

person1 = Person("Mark", "Rogers")

teacher1 =Teacher("Anna", "White")

person1.greet()
teacher1.greet()
```

The screen output will be:

```
Hello! My name is Mark.
Hello! My name is Anna.
```

- In the first line, you created the **class** *Person* with its properties and the *greet* method,

- in line 7, you created the *Teacher* **class**, specifying that it is a child class (of *Person*) with the syntax:

```python
class Derived_Class(Base_Class):
```

  you didn't add any attributes or methods and used the **pass** statement to avoid generating errors,

- in line 9, we created the **object** *person1*, an <u>instance</u> of the *Person* class,

- in line 10, we created the **object** *teacher1*, an <u>instance</u> of the *Teacher* class,

- in lines 11 and 12, both objects execute the *greet* method.

Please note that, while it appears obvious that *person1* has the same attributes and method as the *Person* class, the *teacher1* instance inherits them through the *Teacher* class, which, in turn, had inherited them from the *Person* class.

Now, let's look at a more complex example that will help you better understand the concept of **inheritance** and show how you can use a function and the **if** construct to modify an **object**'s data. We'll provide some comments on the following page.

```python
class Person:

    def __init__(self, name, surname, age, address):
        self.name = name
        self.surname = surname
        self.age = age
        self.address = address

    def show_personal_profile(self):
        profile = f"""
Name = {self.name}
Surname = {self.surname}
Age = {self.age}
Address = {self.address}\n"""
        return profile

    def edit_profile(self):
        print("Edit Profile:
        1 Name
        2 Surname
        3 Age
        4 Address""")
        choice = input("What do you want to edit? ")
    if choice == "1":
        self.name = input("Enter New Name: ")
    elif choice == "2":
        self.surname = input("Enter New Surname: ")
    elif choice == "3":
        self.age = input("Enter New Age: ")
    elif choice == "4":
        self.address = input("Enter New Address: ")

class Student(Person):
    pass
class Teacher(Person):
    pass

student1 = Student("Mark", "Rogers", 21, "New District")
teacher1 = Teacher("Anna", "White", 42, "Old Town")

print(student1.show_personal_profile())
print(teacher1.show_personal_profile())

teacher1.edit_profile()
print(teacher1.show_personal_profile())
```

- Create the *Person* class and

- through the __*init*__ function structure it with four parameters: *Name, Surname, Age* and *Address.*

- Insert the first function (*show_personal_profile)* and note the use of **f-string, triple quotes** and the **newline character** (\n). Also, observe the **return** statement.

- Insert the second function (*edit_profile*) and notice the typical use of the **if** construct associated with the **input** function. This way, an **object** based on this **class** can be modified through prompt.

- Create two child classes (*Student* e *Teacher*) both based on *Person*, without inserting parameters but using the **pass** statement

- Create the **object** *student1* based on the *Student* class. Insert the 4 values *Mark, Rogers, 21* and *New District.* You can do this because the *Student* **class** inherits the structure from the *Person* **class**.

- Create the **object** *teacher1* based on the *Teacher* **class**. This instance will also inherit the structure from *Person*. Insert the 4 values *Anna, White, 42* and *Old Town.*

- Display the personal profile of *student1.*
- Display the personal profile of *teacher1.*

- Call the *edit_profile* function on *teacher1*. Choices are requested, and a property of the instance is modified.

- Display the personal profile of *teacher1*. Note that it has changed.

ADDING ATTRIBUTES

So far, the *Student* and *Teacher* classes do nothing more than replicate the *Person* class, but we've mentioned that a **child class** can also modify or extend the properties and methods of the **parent class**.

Let's write some lines of code to better define the *Student* class

```
Class Student(Person):
    profile = "Student"

    def __init__(self, name, surname, age, address, course):
        super().__init__(name, surname, age, address)
        self.course = course
```

and the *Teacher* class

```
Class Teacher(Person):
    profile = "Teacher"

    def __init__(self, name, surname, age, address, subjects):
        super().__init__(name, surname, age, address)
        self.subjects = subjects
```

Let's see how we've extended both classes by adding to each one an attribute and a professional role:

- each of the two classes has its own *profile*: *Student* or, precisely, *Teacher*,

- in both, we've inserted an __init__ method that includes five attributes: *name*, *surname*, *age*, *address*, and *course* (in the case of *Student*) or *subjects* (in the case of *Teacher*),

- the **super()** function delegates the handling of the first four attributes to the **base class** *Person*,

- in the next line, the fifth attribute is managed, which is an extension of the attributes of the **base class**, *course* (in the case of *Student*) or *subjects* (in the case of *Teacher*).

When creating instances *student1* and *teacher1*, you will add the new attribute:

```
student1 = Student("Mark", "Rogers", 21, "New District", "Antique History")
teacher1 = Teacher("Anna", "White", 42, "Old Town", "Philosophy")
```

L'

OVERRIDING

Let's take a further step and overwrite the function *show_personal_profile* in the two **derived classes**; this process is called **overriding**: when a method in a child class, already belonging to the parent class, is rewritten.

For the *Student* class, you could write:

```python
def show_personal_profile(self):
    profile = f"""
    Profile = {Student.profile}
    Course: {self.course}\n"""
    return super().show_personal_profile() + profile
```

The screen output will be:

```
Name = Mark
Surname = Rogers
Age = 21
Address = New District
Profile: Student
Course: Antique History
```

For the *Teacher* class, you could write:

```python
def show_personal_profile(self):
    profile = f"""
    Profile = {Teacher.profile}
    Subjects Taught: {self.subjects}\n"""
    return super().show_personal_profile() + profile
```

The screen output will be:

```
Name = Anna
Surname = White
Age = 42
Address = Old Town
Profile: Teacher
Subjects Taught: Philosophy
```

TRY EXCEPT

The **try / except** construct allows for intercepting and handling one or more errors during the execution of a code block through **exception handling**, preventing the running program from crashing.

In the following example:

- in line 1, you assign a value to the variable x,

- in line 2 and subsequent lines, the **try** block allows us to test a code block for potential errors,

- in line 4 and subsequent lines, the **except** block allows us to handle the error.

Example:

```
x = 15
try:
    print(x)
except:
    print("The variable x does not exist.")
```

If there is a line 1 (if x exists), line 3 will be displayed on the screen:

`15`

If you remove line 1 (x does not exist), line 5 will be displayed on the screen:

`The variable x does not exist.`

In both cases, the program continues to run.

MULTIPLE EXCEPTION

You can also include multiple **except** clauses to handle various errors.

```
try:
    code block
except error1:
    statement1
except error2:
    statement2
except
    statement3
else
    statement4
finally
    statement5
```

In this case:

- If the `code block` generates an error,

    corresponding to `error1`: then `statement1` will be executed

    corresponding to `error2`: then `statement2` will be executed
- If it generates any other error, `statement3` will be executed
- If no errors occur, `statement4` will be executed
- In any case, `statement5` will also be executed

See examples on the next page.

Note that **try** checks for errors (exceptions) sequentially.

The most common exceptions include: AttributeError, KeyError, IndexError, NameError, TypeError, ValueError, ZeroDivisionError, FileNotFoundError, OSError. For the detailed analysis of each, refer to the Python documentation.

Examples with **multiple exception**.

If the code is executed as written,

```
x = 15

try:
    print(x)
    #print(x[1])
    #print(x.upper())
```

```
except NameError:
    print("Variable x does not exist.")

except TypeError:
    print("Inappropriate object.")

except:
    print("Different type error.")

else:
    print("All good, no errors.")

finally:
    print("Yet, today is a beautiful day.")
```

print(x) will be displayed; *else* will be displayed; *finally* will always be displayed:

```
15
All good, no errors.
Yet, today is a beautiful day.
```

If you remove line 1:

```
#x = 15

try:
    print(x)
    #print(x[1])
    #print(x.upper())
```

print(x) raises the *NameError*, and the code in its corresponding *except* block is executed; *finally* will always be displayed:

```
Variable x does not exist.
Yet, today is a beautiful day.
```

If you delete line 3 and restore line 4:

```
x = 15

try:
    #print(x)
    print(x[1])
    #print(x.upper())
```

$print(x[1])$ raises a $TypeError$, and the code in its corresponding $except$ block is executed; $finally$ will always be displayed:

```
Inappropriate object.
```
```
Yet, today is a beautiful day.
```

If you delete line 4 and restore line 5:

```
x = 15

try:
    #print(x)
    #print(x[1])
    print(x.upper())
```

$print(x.upper())$ generates a different error ($AttributeError$), the code in the third $except$ block is executed; $finally$ will always be displayed:

```
Different type error.
```
```
Yet, today is a beautiful day.
```

RAISE

The **raise** statement allows manually raising an exception, which must then be handled with an **except** or it will cause the program to crash. It can be very useful during the *debugging* phase of your code to understand and resolve potential issues.

Example:

```python
try:
    x = 10
    if x > 5:
        raise ValueError("x is greater than 5.")

except ValueError as error:
    print(f"There has been an error: {error}")
```

If *x* is greater than 5, you will raise the *ValueError* exception and handle it with **except**.

The screen output will be:

```
There has been an error: x is greater than 5.
```

MODULES

A **module** is an external file that contains definitions and instructions. Modules allow you to organize your code by dividing it into multiple files that can be reused in different projects. The file name is the module's name with the **.py** extension.

Example:

Let's say we are working in the **main.py** file and we create a second file called **mymodule.py**.

In **mymodule.py** you write:

```
def greet(name):
    print("Hello, my name is " + name + "!")
```

In **main.py** you write:

```
import mymodule
mymodule.greet("Mark")
```

The screen output will be:

```
Hello, my name is Mark!
```

REMEMBER:
*Usually, modules have names of two or three letters at most. You can create an **alias** for your module when importing it using the syntax:*

```
import mymodule as mm
```

You can add a simple dictionary to the **module**:

```
def greet(name):
    print("Hello, my name is " + name + "!")

person = {
    "name" : "Mark",
    "surname" : "Rogers",
    "age" : 25
    }
```

While in the **main** file, you associate the variable *x* with the value *name* (that is, *Mark*) and pass it to the *greet* function in **mymodule**.

```
import mymodule

x = mymodule.person["name"]
mymodule.greet(x)
```

The screen output will be:

```
Hello, my name is Mark!
```

It is also possible to import a **module** only partially. In the following example, you will import only the list *person* from **mymodule** and display it on the screen.

```
from mymodule import person
print(person)
```

The screen output will be:

```
{'name' : 'Mark', 'surname' : 'Rogers', 'age' : 25}
```

BUILT-IN MODULES

Python contains approximately 200 **built-in modules** that provide a wide range of functionalities, including access to files and directories, data compression, mathematical operations, and more...

The most commonly used ones are:

Os – Allows performing various operations on the operating system.

Math – Enables the use of more complex mathematical functions.

Random – Implements pseudo-random number generators.

Time – Provides various time-related functions.

and others.

They can be imported like any other module, without the need for any installation.

The **dir()** function displays all the functions of a given module passed as an argument.

Example:

```
import math
print(dir(math))
```

As an example, on the next page, we will provide a comprehensive overview of the **datetime** module.

DATES

The **datetime** module is used to parse, format, and perform mathematical operations on dates.

After importing it

```python
import datetime
```

we can obtain the current date and time:

```python
x = datetime.datetime.now()
print(x)
```

It returns the current date and time in the format *[yy]-[mm]-[dd] [hh]:[mm]:[ss].fraction of a second.*

You can also obtain specific date and time:

```python
x = datetime.datetime(2023,2,6,14,50,0)
print(x)
```

Returns:

```
2023-02-06 14:50:00
```

The **strftime()** function formats a date object.

Example:

```python
x = datetime.datetime(2023,2,6,14,50,0)
print(x.strftime("%d %B %y"))
```

And it accepts the following format codes as arguments:

CODE	DESCRIPTION
%a	Abbreviated day name of the week
%A	Full day name of the week
%b	Abbreviated month name
%B	Full month name
%c	Preferred representation of date and time
%C	Century (year divided by 100 and truncated to a decimal integer [00,99])
%d	Day of the month (01-31)
%D	Equivalent to %m/%d/%y
%e	Day of the month (01-31)
%f	Microsecond (000000-999999)
%F	Equivalent to %Y-%m-%d (ISO 8601 date format)
%g	Year without century as a decimal number with leading zeros (00-99)
%G	Year with century as a decimal number
%h	Equivalent to %b
%H	Hour (00-23)
%I	Hour (01-12)
%j	Day of the year (001-366)
%m	Month (01-12)
%M	Minutes(00-59)
%n	Newline character
%p	AM or PM
%r	12-hour clock time (e.g., 11:11:04 PM)
%R	24-hour clock time format (e.g., 23:11)
%S	Seconds (00-61)
%t	Tab character
%T	24-hour clock time (e.g., 23:11:04)
%u	Day of the week as a decimal number (1-7, Monday is 1)
%U	Week number of the year (Sunday as the first day of the week)
%V	ISO week number
%w	Day of the week as a decimal number (0-6, Sunday is 0)
%W	Week number of the year (Monday as the first day of the week)
%x	Preferred representation of date without time
%X	Preferred representation of time without date
%y	Year without century as a decimal number (00-99)
%Y	Year with century as a decimal number
%z	Time zone offset
%Z	Time zone name or abbreviation
%%	A literal '%' character.

Note: codes may vary depending on the version and platform used.

PIP

PIP (an acronym for Pip Installs Packages), is a command-line tool that allows the installation of packages designed for Python, enabling additional functionalities.

To verify that PIP is correctly installed – it is provided during the installation of Python – open the shell and type `pip -version`.

You should see a line like:

```
pip 22.3.1 from C:\Program Files\Python311\Lib\site-packages\pip (python 3.11)
```

Once you have selected the package of interest, by connecting to the `pypi.org` site,

you can install it using the syntax:

```
pip install packagename
```

To uninstall it, the syntax would be:

```
pip uninstall packagename
```

To get a list of all installed packages, the syntax is:

```
pip list
```

To use the functionalities of the newly installed package in your program, it is sufficient to import it like any other module:

```
import namepackage
```

It is advisable to have a general idea of the available packages so that you are aware of them when looking for the most efficient solutions for your code.

WORKING WITH FILES

File handling holds significant importance in programming, and Python allows you to **create**, **open**, and **close** files, as well as perform operations on them.

To open a file, you use the **open()** function with the following syntax:

```
open("filename","mode").
```

There are four modes:

R (*read*): reads a file – returns an error if it doesn't exist.

A (*append*): appends information to the file – creates it if it doesn't exist.

W (*write*): writes to the file – creates it if it doesn't exist.

X (*create*): creates a file – returns an error if it already exists.

To follow the examples below, in PyCharm, create a file (*file.txt*) by right-clicking on main.py, selecting new from the menu, and choosing file.

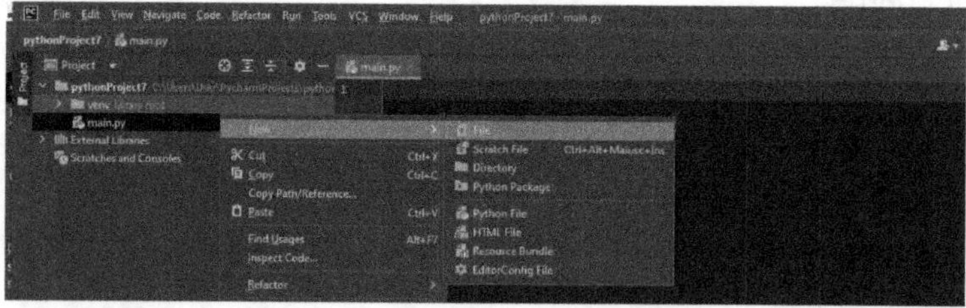

In the dialog box that opens, type the file name (*file.txt*). It will be added as a new tab.

Write the following three lines in your file:

To be, or not to be, that is the question:

Whether 'tis nobler in the mind to suffer

The slings and arrows of outrageous fortune,

Reading a file.

By passing the **"r"** (*read*) parameter to **open()**, the **read()** method reads the content of a file.

Example:

```
f = open("file.txt", "r")
print(f.read())
f.close()
```

Returns:

```
To be, or not to be, that is the question:
Whether 'tis nobler in the mind to suffer
The slings and arrows of outrageous fortune,
```

In line 3 you used the **close()** method to close the file and release the associated resources.

Read part of the file.

Specify a number of characters.

Example:

```
f = open("file.txt", "r")
print(f.read(5))
```

Returns:

```
To be
```

Read one or more lines:

The **readline()** method reads a line of characters, including the end-of-line character, which is the \n character.

Example:

```
f = open("file.txt", "r")
print(f.readline())
```

Returns:

```
To be, or not to be, that is the question:
```

To read the subsequent lines, we can repeat the statement `print(f.readline())`

```
f = open("file.txt", "r")
print(f.readline())
print(f.readline())
print(f.readline())
```

Oppure possiamo usare un ciclo **for**:

```
f = open("file.txt", "r")
for line in f:
    print(line)
```

In both cases, the result will be:

```
To be, or not to be, that is the question:
Whether 'tis nobler in the mind to suffer
The slings and arrows of outrageous fortune,
```

Note that it is not possible to read the content of the file if it is not opened with the **"r"** parameter.

Write to the file (append).

By passing the "**a**" parameter (*append*) to **open()**, the **write()** method writes to the end of the file.

Example:

```
f = open("file.txt", "a")
f.write(" I am writing here.")
```

Il contenuto del file cambierà in:

To be, or not to be, that is the question:

Whether 'tis nobler in the mind to suffer

The slings and arrows of outrageous fortune, I am writing here.

Write to the file (overwrite).

By passing the "**w**" parameter (*write*) to **open()**, the **write()** method overwrites the content of the file.

Es:

```
f = open("file.txt", "w")
f.write("I am writing here.")
```

The content of the file will change to:

I am writing here.

Modify the file.

To modify the content of a file, you can use a procedure similar to what you have seen for modifying tuples.

- Open the file in read mode,
- Put the content, or part of it, into a variable,
- Make the desired changes,
- Overwrite the file using the **write()** method.

In the following example, we will take the entire file and rewrite it in uppercase characters:

```
f = open("file.txt", "r")
text = f.read()
text = text.upper()
f = open("file.txt", "w")
f.write(text)
```

The content of the file will change to:

TO BE, OR NOT TO BE, THAT IS THE QUESTION:

WHETHER 'TIS NOBLER IN THE MIND TO SUFFER

THE SLINGS AND ARROWS OF OUTRAGEOUS FORTUNE,

Creating a new file.

To create a file, as we saw at the beginning of the chapter, we can pass the **"x"** parameter (*create*) to the **open()** function. However, it's worth noting that also the **"w"** and **"a"** parameters create a new file if they don't find an existing one.

Deleting a file.

To delete a file, we need to import the **OS** module and use the syntax

```
os.remove("file_path")
```

Example:

```
import os
os.remove("file.txt")
```

Since removing a non-existent file generates an error, it will often be useful to perform a check.

Example:

```
import os
if os.path.exists("file.txt"):
    os.remove("file.txt")
```

JSON

JSON (JavaScript Object Notation) is a textual format for representing structured data. It allows the aggregation of strings, numbers, etc. to create real **objects**, commonly used for exchanging information between a web server and a client application. **JSON** data consists of key-value pairs and can be easily parsed and used by various platforms and programming languages.

We can compare it, with some differences, to a **dictionary**.

Example:

```
{
"name" : "Mark",
"surname" : "Rogers",
"age" : 21,
"profile" : "Teacher",
"address" : {
    "street" : "Church, 18",
    "city" : "Rome"
}
}
```

Let's see how to handle a **JSON** object in the Python language. In the following example, you will convert it into a **dictionary**:

```python
import json

j = '{"name" : "Mark", "surname" : "Rogers", "age" : 25, "job" : "Teacher"}'
y = json.loads(j)

print(type(y))
print(y)
```

- In line 1, you imported the appropriate json module.

- In line 2, you assigned the data of your object to *j*, noting that you used **single quotes** to delimit it.

- In line 3, you used **loads()** to assign the object to *y*. The **json.loads()** function converts a string into a **dictionary**.

- In line 4, you perform a test and, indeed, it returns: `<class 'dict'>`.

- In line 5, you print *y*.

In the next example, you will do the opposite:

```python
j = {
    "name" : "Mark",
    "surname" : "Rogers",
    "age" : 25,
    "profile" : "Teacher"
}

y = json.dumps(j)

print(type(y))
print(y)
```

- In line 1 and following, you create a **dictionary** with your data.

- In line 7, you use **dumps()** to convert the dictionary. The **json.dumps()** function converts any data into a string in **JSON** format.

- In line 8, you perform a test, and indeed, it returns: `<class 'str'>`.

- In line 9, you print *y*

and you will obtain:

```
{"name": "Mark", "surname": "Rogers", "age": 25, "profile": "Teacher"}
```

FORMATTING AND SORTING JSON

Indent is an argument of **dumps()** that makes the string more readable.
With the syntax `y = json.dumps(j, indent = 4)`

the same string would appear as follows:

```
{
    "name": "Mark",
    "surname": "Rogers",
    "age": 25,
    "profile": "Teacher"
}
```

Separators allows you to replace the *comma* and *colon* separators with custom strings.
With the syntax `y = json.dumps(j, separators=("/", "="))`

the same string would appear as follows:

```
{"name"="Mark"/"surname"="Rogers"/"age"=25/"profile"="Teacher"}
```

Sort_keys arranges the keys of the string in alphabetical order.
With the syntax `y = json.dumps(j, sort_keys=True)`

the same string would appear as follows:

```
{"surname": "Rogers", "age": 25, "name": "Mark", "profile": "Teacher"}
```

It is recommended, to become familiar with writing JSON objects, to practice with the numerous existing *online parsing* sites.

The Elements Of Python

Argento Publishing